KB218506

The Red Shoes

Hans Christian Andersen

Retold by Rob Waring
Illustrated by Alice Sinkner

Series Editor Rob Waring

☀ Introduction ☀

This is a story by Hans Christian Andersen.

It is a story about a girl who doesn't listen to others.

☀ Characters ☀

Karen

Old Woman

Angel

☀ Words to Know ☀

broken

church

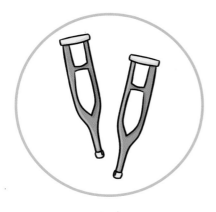

crutches

rose

Karen is a poor girl.
She lives with an old woman.

Karen asks the old woman for
some red dancing shoes.

5

Karen wears the red shoes to church.

"Red shoes are not for church,"
others say.
Karen does not listen.

Karen goes to a dance.
The shoes start dancing.

Karen cannot stop the shoes from dancing. They dance and dance.

The shoes take her to the forest.
The shoes take her to the mountains.
The shoes dance for many days.
Karen is very tired.
She cannot sleep.

Karen takes off her shoes, but her legs are broken.
Now she walks with crutches.

Karen goes to church.
She wants to say sorry.
The red shoes stop her from going
to church.

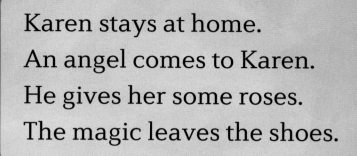

Karen stays at home.
An angel comes to Karen.
He gives her some roses.
The magic leaves the shoes.

Karen is now free from
the red shoes.
She can go to church
and say sorry.

✳ Playlet ✳

The Red Shoes
Hans Christian Andersen

Cast   Karen, Old Woman, Man, Woman, Angel

Scene   **In a small town**

The old woman and Karen are walking in the town.

Karen: I like those shoes. Please buy them.

Old Woman: No, Karen. You can't have them.

Karen: Please!

The old woman buys the shoes for Karen. Then Karen goes to church.

Woman: Red shoes in church? No!

Man: No red shoes in church.

Karen goes to a party. The shoes start to dance.

Karen: Oh, my shoes. They are dancing.

Karen dances and dances. She wants to stop.

Karen: Stop dancing, shoes!

The shoes do not stop dancing. They take her into the forest.

Karen: Please stop dancing. I'm so tired.

The shoes do not stop dancing.

Karen: My feet! My feet! I will take off my shoes.

Karen takes off the shoes.

Karen: Oh no! My feet! They are broken. I cannot walk now.

Karen goes to church on crutches.
The shoes stop her from going in the church.

Karen: Shoes, stop dancing. I want to go to church.

Karen goes home to her room. The angel comes into the room.

Karen: Who are you? Are you an angel?

Angel: Take these roses. They will stop the magic shoes.

Karen takes the roses.

Karen: Thank you, Angel.

Karen goes to church. The shoes are by the church door, but they are not dancing.

Karen: The shoes are not dancing! I can go to church. Next time, I will listen.

The End

✳ Story Review ✳

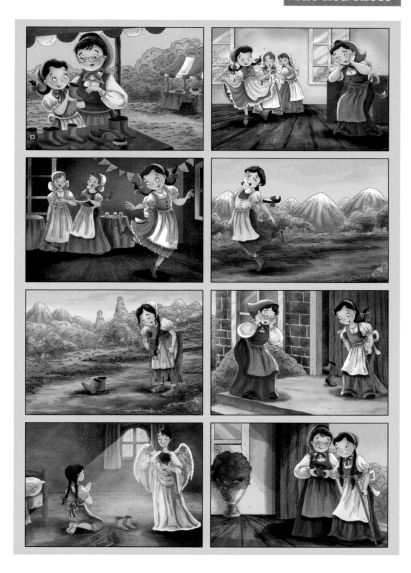

e-future Classic Readers Level S

Levels	Starter	1	2	3	4	5	6
CEFR	A1	A1	A1	A1	A1/A2	A2	A2
Headwords	200	250	350	550	800	1000	1300